My First
Travel Book

This book belongs to:

....

From:

Coplen Falie

....

Date:

8/10/15

....

Signed by:

Nkls

....

My First Travel Books

The Seven Natural Wonders of The Earth

with

Captain

Frankie

Anna Othitis

My First Travel Books

The Seven Natural Wonders of the Earth

© Anna Othitis 2014

ISBN: 978-1499190281

ALL RIGHTS RESERVED.

Cover design and image editing by Cecelia Morgan

Editing and Formatting by LionheART Publishing House, part of LionheART Galleries Ltd

A special thank you to my son, Frankie Othitis, "Captain Frankie".

He is a pilot and has provided me with the inspiration and encouragement to continue authoring children's books. It is a pleasure to create this wonderful series of *My First Travel Books* with more adventurous travels on our amazing "Angelic Airlines".

To my husband, George, and sons, Johnny and Elia, thank you for your wonderful encouragement, inspiration, praise and support at all times. You are all such shining stars of love and affection in my life.

Of course a big thank you to my wonderful little readers for your support and expressive imaginations.

Thank You All So Much

Welcome aboard Angelic Airlines. This is your Captain Frankie, and I will be flying you to more popular destinations around the world. This time we will be visiting our 'Original Seven Wonders of the Earth'.

Please fasten your seat belts, stow your bags, make yourselves comfortable and get ready for a smooth take off on another wondrous journey into the deep blue skies.

The Beautiful Colorful Country Flags of the Seven Wonders of Our World

Iceland

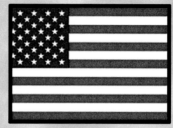

United Sates of America

Mexico

Brazil

Australia

Nepal

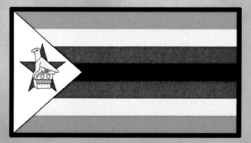

Zimbabwe

This is a map of our world which shows where you can find our original Seven Wonders. What a big world we live in, so wide and spread over the oceans.

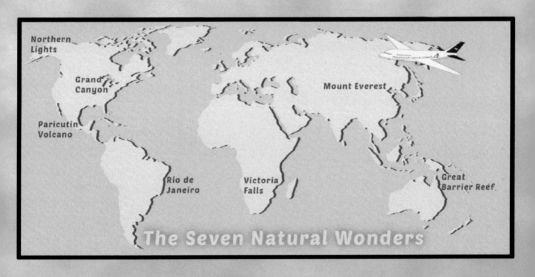

Northern Lights

Grand Canyon

Paricutin Volcano

Mount Everest

Rio de Janeiro

Victoria Falls

Great Barrier Reef

The Seven Natural Wonders

The Northern Lights in the Arctic and Antarctic

Look at the flaming lights shining high in the sky,
like beautiful colored party ribbons they stretch and
curve as we fly.
Waving like dancing figures, jumping left to right,
they show off their brightness in the
darkness of night.
Clashing together, the colors so bold.
Blue, green, pink and red story is told.
So light and so bright telling of their love and pride,
what an amazing natural wonder, another glorious
airplane ride!

The energy of the Aurora are the particles in solar winds clashing together and going past the Earth.

This shows beautiful different colors of light that are reflected off the white snow in the north and south poles.

These lights can be seen in the North Arctic and South Antarctic, Iceland, Alaska and Northern Canada.

When the sun peeps up to rise in the sky, a greenish or faint red glow can be seen.

In what countries can you see the Northern lights?

Where is the Arctic pole? Is it in the north or south of the Earth?

Where is the Antarctic Pole? Is it in the north or the south of the Earth?

Name some of the colors of the Northern Lights.

Grand Canyon In Colorado, USA

Our next destination to visit is the deep Grand Canyon.

The majestic colorful rocks making up the beautiful canyon site,

stand like a range of brave soldiers with great power and great might.

The eagles and birds soar through like darts,

like kites they glide gracefully until the sunset starts.

The Grand Canyon is huge, high and long, with steep, sharp colorful cliffs of red rock. The Colorado River in Arizona, USA twists for miles and miles through these famous rocky mountains.

To the Native American Indians it has been sacred ground for centuries.

The Grand Canyon is one hundred and seventy miles long, eighteen miles wide and one mile deep. The ancient rocks form different layers of red colors and have kept their steep shape for thousands of years.

This wonder is home to many different kinds of animals and plants. Animals such as snakes, coyotes, fish and bears all have their homes here. Prickly cacti can also be found in the canyon. A lot of people travel to the Grand Canyon each year to go hiking and camping.

In which country is the Grand Canyon?

What is the name of the river that twists through the mountains?

What lives in the caves of the Grand Canyon?

What are the names of the prickly plants on the steep hills?

Paricutin Volcano in Mexico

As we fly over this mountain, a huge deep hole
on the top,
with bellowing smoke, at any moment it could pop.
Let's fly around and land a good distance away,
a destination so beautiful but can erupt at any
time of day.
The thick red glowing magma sits waiting its turn,
to shoot out of the top and anything in its
path burn.

The Paricutin Volcano is a cinder cone volcano that grew quickly in a cornfield. Its lava can rise to about fifty feet below the crater's edge. The Paricutin volcano now stands at exactly one thousand three hundred and fifty three feet, which is taller than the Empire State Building in New York City.

The type of eruption that happens is called a Strombolian eruption, and hot lava explodes from a single open hole at the top of a volcano.

Paricutin is about two hundred miles west of Mexico City, in the state of Michoacán, Mexico. Paricutin is part of the Volcanic Axis "The Transversal", meaning that it is part of a line of many volcanoes. Paricutin was named after a small Tarascan Indian village.

In which country is the Paricutin Volcano?

What is the type of the eruption called?

What do the sparks of the boiling fire remind you of?

What is the red hot mud that flows over of the volcano called?

The Harbor Of Rio de Janeiro – Brazil

Now fasten your seat belts and let's visit yet another natural wonder, the harbor of Rio de Janeiro, the biggest natural harbor in the world.

Like giant ant hills, huge mountains surround
the bay.

Like hundreds of ants, ships come in and out
every day.

The statue of Christ the Redeemer stands with his
arms reaching out,

greeting people who visit and the ones
who live about.

The harbor is located around Rio de Janeiro, Brazil. It is the largest natural bay in the world and is surrounded by granite stone mountains formed by the erosion of the Atlantic Ocean, also called the Guanabara Bay. What a wonder!

The Portuguese people who found this bay called it "The River of January". The famous Sugarloaf Mountain stands tall at one thousand two hundred and ninety six feet high.

The Corcovado Peak is two thousand two hundred and ninety nine feet high, with the hills of Tijuca at three thousand three hundred and fifty feet. The views are magnificent from these mountains with the famous monument overlooking the bay.

In which country is this large natural harbor?

On what does the big statue stand?

What does the statue of Christ the Redeemer wear?

What ocean water runs into the large harbor?

The Great Barrier Reef In Australia

Even though we fly high, we fly over the
"Down Under".

Off the shore of the land there are so
many wonders.

Now, children, look down at the fish in the sea,

so many different colors, and sizes, they all
look so free.

The coral reef their home, a natural
wildlife preserve,

such precious value it holds to our Earth, something
we need to conserve.

The Great Barrier Reef can actually be seen from outer space. It is the largest coral reef in the world and is surrounded by hundreds of islands and thousands of coral reefs. The native Australian Aborigine call this their spiritual ground.

Over one thousand five hundred species of fish of all colors and sizes can be found here, including many unusual and funny looking types of fish like the colorful clownfish, angelfish and butterfly fish. Other animals such as birds, sea turtles, sharks, whales, sea snakes and so much more live here. There are two million fish living in this great reef.

The corals have wonderful beautiful colors and cannot be removed from the water. Coral is a soft-bodied, invertebrate animal, having no backbone.

In the year of 1981 the Great Barrier Reef was selected as a World Heritage Site.

Where is the Great Barrier Reef?

What animals can you find in the deep blue sea?

Is the Great Barrier Reef the largest in the World?

What is coral made of?

Victoria Falls – Zimbabwe

As every running river flows, this one comes
to a fall,

standing hundreds of feet high like a mighty
water wall.

Almost year round, the falls make their loud sound,

rolling over the cliff top and straight to the ground.

The Victoria Falls water drops three hundred and fifty four feet down. The spray can be seen from miles away and the Africans named the falls 'The Smoke that Thunders'.

After the water plunges to the base, it flows into the Batoka Gorge. The falls mark the border between two African countries: Zimbabwe and Zambia. Victoria Falls is known to be one of our world's Natural Wonders for its deepest and largest cliff drops.

The falls are at their strongest strength in April when the rainy season is at its peak.

Why are the Victoria Falls a wonder of the world?

What do the African people call these falls?

Into which river does the water run?

Into which gorge does the water fall?

Mount Everest - Himalayas

It's the highest part of our Earth, the grandest
of grand.

Mount Everest is the tallest naturally made
mountain in all of our land.

The clouds in the air lurk like mist in the night,

but flow peacefully through the valleys, it's quite
a nice sight.

With the different shades of blue and its peaks
snow-covered in white,

this mountain has existed since the beginning of
darkness and light.

The name of this wondrous mountain means "goddess of the sky" or "goddess of the universe".

Mount Everest is in Mahalangur, Himalayas, and is the highest mountain on the Earth with the unbelievable height of over twenty nine thousand feet. These mountains are shared by the two Asian countries of China and Nepal and many people visit to climb this famous mountain because of its height.

Cold weather and low oxygen are two of the dangers that the height of Everest produces. We are lucky that our airplane helps make the oxygen that we need to fly as high as Mount Everest.

What floats through the mountains?

Where are the Himalaya mountains?

What people visit this famous mountain?

Why is it dangerous to be so high up on the mountain?

Captain Frankie's Quiz Question

Children, do you know which are the

Seven NATURAL Wonders of the Earth?

Speak them out loud with me:

The Northern Lights

The Grand Canyon

The Paricutin Volcano

The Harbor of Rio de Janeiro

The Great Barrier Reef

The Victoria Falls

Mount Everest

Girls and boys, this once again brings us to the end of our wonderful journey traveling to our Natural Wonders of the Earth. I hope that you had a fun and pleasant flight. I thank you for flying with me on Angelic Airlines. We got to see and learn about more wonderful wonders on our Earth.

Let us look after our world and its environment to preserve these wonders.
We will be back soon with more
Angelic Airline Adventures

Stay on board with your Captain Frankie.
I hope to see you all again very soon and I always welcome you aboard.

"We Are The World, We Are The People Living In It"

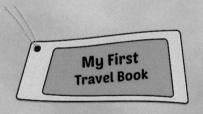

My First
Travel Book

Children, here is your boarding pass and airplane ticket for Our Next World Travel

SEE YOU SOON AND REMEMBER, TAKE CARE OF OUR EARTH

More Angelic Airline Adventures coming soon, with your friendly Captain Frankie.